Under the Sign of the Lily

The Messianic
Sophianic Age

I Pray unto
the Power of Love

The eternal word,
the One God, the Free Spirit,
speaks through Gabriele,
as through all the prophets of God—
Abraham, Job, Moses, Elijah, Isaiah,
Jesus of Nazareth,
the Christ of God

I Pray unto the Power of Love

Christ, the Son of God
and Co-Regent of the Kingdom of God,
gave a revelation in September 2021
through the prophetess
and emissary of God, Gabriele

"I Pray unto the Power of Love"

1st Edition March 2022
©Gabriele-Verlag Das Wort GmbH
Max-Braun-Str. 2, 97828 Marktheidenfeld
www.gabriele-verlag.com
www.gabriele-publishing-house.com

Translated from the original German title:

„Ich bete an die Macht der Liebe"

The German edition is the work of reference
for all question regarding the meaning of the content.
All decorative letters: © Gabriele-Verlag Das Wort
All rights reserved
Order No. S 199en

Printed by: KlarDruck GmH, Markheidenfeld, Germany

ISBN 978-3-96446-241-1

I Pray unto the Power of Love

Gabriele introduces the word of revelation of the Christ of God:

God is the love; He speaks to you—through every flower, through every blade of grass, through every animal, through all of nature. God speaks through every ray of sun, through a breath of wind; each drop of water contains a thousandfold power. God is love, indeed, He is the omnipresent love. God is in every soul and in every ensouled human being. God is in every cell of the physical body, every component of the body is vivified by His power.

Many of my fellow people near and far, I almost want to say, all over the world, know that I, Gabriele, have been receiving His eternal word for nearly five decades and that since then, the Eternal, His Son Christ and the Cherub of the third basic power before God's throne have been giving revelations through me, the prophetess of God. How I was called to this task is described in the book, *"A Woman's Life in Service of the Eternal."*

Dear fellow people, many years ago, an acquaintance gave me the text of a song, which, for me, Gabriele, became words of the adoration of God.

The words of this song accompanied me into the day. They became for me the guidance to God in me and to the Christ of God, to His Sermon on the Mount.

Perhaps these words in the text "I Pray unto the Power of Love" also want to say something to you. To me, they stand for the truth. The text reads:

"I pray unto the power of love,
that reveals itself in Christ above;
I yield unto the noble impulse,
with which as child I have been loved.
I want, in place of selfish thinking,
to let myself in seas of love be sinking.

How favorably you're disposed toward me,
and how my heart longs so for You!
With love that strongly, gently draws me,
all my being bows unto You!
You intimate love, You kind being,
You have chosen me, and I have chosen You.

O Christ, that Your name be imprinted,
deeply engraved in this mine heart!
May Your true love and brotherly kindness,
be stamped for always in heart and sense!
In word, in deed, in every being,
may it be Christ, and none other to be read.

Until today, the lines of this song have become for me the adoration of the All-One God, the Father-Mother-God, whom I love and who is instruction and home for me.

One evening, as I sat in my prayer corner praying to the Eternal All-One God, I just happened, as they say, to pick up the words of the song, that is, the words of adoration. Although the words, that is, the text, of the song were and are more than familiar to me, I began to read. I read the first four lines, and suddenly, I felt as if I could read no further.

I paused, for I had the divine prophetic word and knew that the Eternal now had something to say to me—and indeed, something was said to me. It began:

I Am the Am, the Christ of God, the Son of the All-One Eternal God, of the Father-Mother-Being of all His sons and daughters.

Verily, I Am in God, My Father, who is the Father of all divine beings and of all souls and ensouled human beings.

Through the Eternal All-One and through the Cherub of Wisdom in God and in unity with his dual, it is evident that homebringing is announced.

The homebringing through the Eternal All-One God not only applies to all souls—God's love also stimulates ensouled people to reflect.

In the same development, that is, cycle, the recovery of the density of the substance called matter is also called for because it, too, becomes subject to refinement.

Everything will be raised again to the primordial substance, to fine materiality. Therefore, the word "recovery."

As Jesus of Nazareth, I said to the souls and ensouled people: "I come soon."

What I promised as Jesus of Nazareth, "I come soon," I will make true as Christ.

In this awareness, I addressed the supporting pair of divine Wisdom, the third basic power before God's throne, who, without hesitation, placed their Yes into My promise: "I come soon."

The yes had content, in which the promise was given expression. The dual principle in unity with the Father-Mother-God and with Me, His Son, immediately began to set the course for this.

One heavenly messenger, one prophet of God after another, took on an incarnation and spoke the word of the I Am the I Am from the Spirit, in the respective language of their time.

In this awareness, the primordial bearer of divine Wisdom also came, which says, one in primordial unity with the primordial Being of love.

Thus it was, and so it is:

God, the Eternal, spoke in many divine revelations about time and about the quantum of creating and drawing Light-Ether, which was granted to the renegade beings as a loan, since they wanted to prove that they could fashion a better creation than God, the Eternal. Mind you: It was merely a loan.

Times upon times have passed, and that means: Energies upon energies have been used up, the so-called zero point, in terms of used up energy, has been reached. This means that time, the loan, has expired—it is over.

Up to the so-called zero point in terms of the loan, countless messengers of God came.

The last messenger of God is a woman, as humankind has heard. She is the Seraph of divine Wisdom, in unity with her spirit dual, the Cherubim, spoken in a short earthly word as "Cherub." Both were once called by Me, the Christ of God, to prepare the way that began almost 2000 years ago with My word as Jesus of Nazareth: "I come soon."

Since that time, the supporting pair of the law-power of divine Wisdom, Cherub and Seraph, have been working together.

The female principle began the path of incarnations and the male principle accompanied her. Before the incarnation of Jesus of Nazareth, the Cherub, the male principle, was in the earthly garment, and thus, a human being, in order to announce, as a prophet of God, the coming of Jesus of Nazareth, with words that also announced His work as the Christ of God after the time of Jesus of Nazareth, the Messiah—of course, with the words of the time in which the Cherub was incarnated.

Looked at and listened to, the content of this New Era comes to life. Without searching for long, the answer is: "I come soon."

Since Jesus of Nazareth, My words resound again and again: "I come soon." For almost 2000 years, the Seraph of divine Wisdom, with differing human names, that is, incarnations, and in many different communities, taught the infinitely eternal law of love for God and neighbor and the coming of the Christ of God.

Difficult, not to say most difficult, that is, cruel, times are coming to an end, in which she was accompanied by the Cherub, also called the Prince of Wisdom, in order to prepare the coming of the Christ of God, who I Am. The Eternal All-One God introduced the New Era and the way into the Kingdom of Heaven.

On the way to the Eternal Being, to the Sanctum, there will still be levels and communities, because practice is required, in terms of what it means to be in unity and to be in communication with all living beings, which is the All-language of infinity.

On all the levels leading into the Kingdom of Heaven, into the Sanctum, I, the Christ of God, will take over the continuing guidance, one with the divine Wisdom that is the primordial Wisdom and that directs and guides into the Sanctum, that is active in infinity and is thus, the heavenly standard for the creating and drawing of all beings in infinity.

The time has come: The Eternal and all beings of the Being have triumphed.

The "Let there be" is not merely spoken—Christ and the primordial Wisdom have begun to bring into action the homebringing of all beings more and more, because the "Let there be" is beginning to create the foundation for further realms. This means that the Sanctum sets into motion the energies for this and leads into the respective primordial unity.

Spoken with the words of this world—for the instrument, the divine primordial Wisdom, the Seraph, is still in the temporal in order to translate the word of the heavens:

The Sanctum is the center of the eternal Being. It is the seat of God-Father, of the Christ of God and of the seven princely pairs.

Every spiritual atom, be it ever so small, has the core, the motive power, directed toward the primordial Love and toward the primordial Wisdom.

Every coarse-material structure, also called matter, must be transformed, because every coarse-materiality is base material, base energy, which the adversary thought up that way and laid out for himself. Transience is already inherent in all coarse materiality.

In order to make understandable that "coarse-materiality" is not a part of "fine-materiality," I will try to explain the whole thing via the prophetess of God, Gabriele; for the eternal Being is, after all, eternal, and therefore, not coarse-material.

Every soul will have to go level by level, for there is no death, only transformation, and just as the human beings burden themselves, they also take their path as a soul. No one can take the path for another, even if the act of Redemption is taught differently in the so-called Christian churches. Redemption also means liberation, not from personal guilt, that is, sin, but from death. People do indeed die, but not their burdened entity, also called sin. All of nature is vivified life—there is nothing that humankind can call "death." The time, which the Satanist, that is, Satan, and his kind agreed upon, was merely a loan, which has expired.

The words of the prince of divine Wisdom convey this: "Nothing proven—merely destroyed."

The true, the eternal, life is so manifold that one can speak of many, even countless, levels, that is, realms. Each level into the Eternal Kingdom must be accepted and fulfilled again, in order to return to the Father's house.

With human words, the word "perfection" sounds as if one were speaking of something that has gone very well. In infinity, one speaks of "perfect" as the Eternal is perfect, that is, flawless—that means:

No impure law-radiation, nothing that flows against the intrinsic value, the being in the Being, no tinge, nothing. God is the I Am.

Spoken into this world, to this Earth, this also means: absolute purity, absolute love for God and neighbor, the law of "I Am the I Am."

Up to the Kingdom of Peace this means: work on oneself, work all the way to perfection. Thus, there will be peace then, and the being will be without shadow, that is, flawless. Up to the Kingdom of Peace, there is still more or less shadow—depending on the state of consciousness of the being. Only once the core of being is totally and completely opened, is the being a spirit being. It is perfect. Whatever human words mean or however human beings may interpret "perfection"—the spirit being is the spirit being out of His Spirit, God. The spirit being is not God, but divine.

In the text of the song, which for me has become an adoration of God, it says:

"How favorably you're disposed toward me,
and how my heart longs so for You!
With love that strongly, gently draws me,
all my being bows unto You!
You intimate love, You kind being,
You have chosen me, and I have chosen You."

Christ continued:

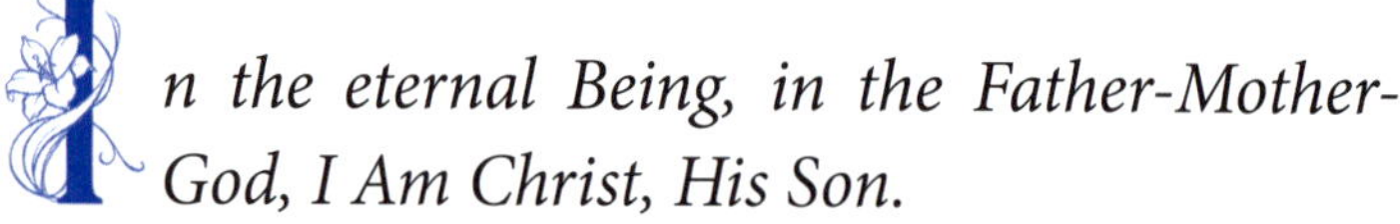

In the eternal Being, in the Father-Mother-God, I Am Christ, His Son.

The New Era begins with the Christ-path into the Kingdom of Peace. The old sinful world is passing away.

Quarrelling, divisiveness, war, murder and manslaughter are the rituals of the old nation. Rape, theft, exploitation and genocide also belong to the old Earth. All is being prepared for transformation and brought to it. Churches, cathedrals, pastors and priests, all reverends and excellencies with their apostolates in church times and the like are also in the process of passing away. They belong to the shadow of the old Earth, which is examined by the New Era solely in order to remember that the human being in the New Era no longer belongs to it.

I Am the Christ of God and the Christ-path into the Kingdom of Peace.

Who will go with Me?
Who dismantles with My power the still active past in themselves and in their being that is still attached to the world here and there?

Everything that is all-too-human is dwindling and should also gradually fade for the wayfarers on the Christ-path to the Kingdom of Peace and move away from them, that is, be discarded by them, in order to surrender it for transformation.

Briefly repeated: For the wayfarers on the Christ-path to the Kingdom of Peace, there should be neither theologians nor priests, no superiors or excellencies such as bishops, cardinals and Holy Fathers, and so forth. For them, there are no stone churches, no cathedrals and no worship services with the corresponding ceremonies, no rosaries, no holy water, no auricular confession, etc.

The first thing that those who believe in My word and confidently walk the Christ-path realize is that they are the temple of God and that the light of neighborly love begins to shine in them.

Once neighborly love is fully developed in the soul, then person and soul have reached the core of being. This means: The person and their soul have overcome this cruel world thus far, since their feeling, thinking and speaking are directed heavenward and the kingdoms of nature feel the word of the human being.

This means work on oneself. Everything else only indicates reincarnation, the desire to continue to be as before and to still take their time for the New Era.

A help for self-examination:

Human beings deceive themselves all too easily. Only once thoughts of desires and wanting fade and come up only now and then as memories—because here and there, the world still is as it is—do people begin to liberate themselves from the wheel of reincarnation. A sign that this is so is the inner perception.

The Eternal Kingdom is based on the infinitely eternal law of love for God and neighbor. All heavenly beings came forth from the all-flowing law of love for God and neighbor.

The all-flowing law of love for God and neighbor is the birthplace of all spirit beings, but also of the All-Being, of the suns, planets, nature kingdoms etc., etc.

That is the aspect "unity"; that is the All-communication of sending and receiving. That is also the Christ-path into the Kingdom of Peace, and beginning with the Kingdom of Peace, into eternity, to the families of the Being.

For many people, this can still be a long way, considering that the majority of people are attached to their ecclesiastical necessities, preached to them by pastors, priests and other ecclesiastical, tabernacle teachers.

Jesus of Nazareth, who I once was as a human being, taught the opposite. My statements as Jesus of Nazareth stand until today in the book of truth, in the law of the love for God and neighbor.

When people were more oriented to church doctrine, then they were, and are, oriented to the law of divide, bind and rule, to traditions and superstition, which means, again and again, to reincarnation, re-embodiment. That is why there will still be light-filled and shadowed places on the planet for long times—for some, who walk the Christ-path, the light-filled places, for the others, the shadowed places, in order to incarnate there, until they recognize the often countless entanglements in ecclesiastical dramaturgies, and expiate them, which also means to take on the suffering of those whom they themselves led astray.

Light and shadow will still exist in alternation for a long time, because those who have abused, and still abuse, My name "Christ" and the term "Christian values" are still many.

Despite all these "fors and againsts," truly God-seeking people will walk the Christ-path to the Kingdom of Peace and increasingly learn what the following means:

Leave behind the old sinfulness, the time of conflict and war against people, animals and the kingdoms of nature.

Repent and clear up your still sinful aspects, and find yourself on the Christ-path. The path to Me and with Me enables you to gain distance from your all-too-human aspect, since your thoughts and words, indeed, your entire behavior on the Christ-path, achieve victory over yourself.

Bit by bit you take in the messages that come from nature. Who is speaking in you? Suddenly a flower or a stone—companions that go with you.

In time, the desolate past falls away from you, all that was in the times of times, for example, years ago, or in earlier reports of war, murder, genocide, of killing animals, slaughtering animals, poisoning fields, cutting down trees and much more.

What is past and what you also clear up in yourself is at first borne as if in a mist; then many an impression fades. However, you begin very gradually to communicate with everything that surrounds you, which means: It sends and you receive.

You are not alone.

More and more Christ-wayfarers to the Kingdom of Peace contact you and live on a purified Earth, cleansed by the Earth's plasma.

What is gradually rising in them is the world of the Christ, as revealed in the spoken and written word, in and on an Earth that the Eternal All-One has cleansed, just as the mists are lifting.

Some may ask:

"As the mists are lifting?"

Yes, it is so.

How does that work?

The Earth, the world, has many junctions; they are called towns, homesteads, villages, communities and not least, cities and countries.

Particularly in countries, the personal warfare continues, including the fighting between countries; the machinery of war may not be ignored.

Few people think about the fact that the Earth is in constant vibration right down into the depths of the oceans, and that here and there the ground rises, from slightly to powerfully. This also means that above the so-called stratosphere—as human beings call it—finer currents build up that are perceived by people who truly walk the Christ-path.

This means that their consciousness is raised and conveys to them a different way of seeing and living, as an image for their life habits.

Either their location changes, or there is even a shift, so as to change further. This can go so far that people join together with like-minded people, thus creating a hamlet; it can also be a larger local area.

This means that the spiritual planet rises here and there and guides the faithful wayfarer on the path, which in many cases can also be just a path of consciousness, for example, by changing one's way of thinking and living.

Carefully, but consciously, I, the Christ, lead the wayfarers on the paths into the Kingdom of Peace. I, Christ, call this guidance, perception via a change of consciousness.

Indeed, the Earth will very gradually change through the upward radiation, that is, the irradiation via the depths of the Earth.

The planet from the Sanctum—I call it the Christ-planet—begins at the root; it takes up the energies of the Earth in order to transform them, because during the steps of transformation toward the Kingdom of Peace, the planet moves on to its primordial location, the Sanctum, which means, into primordial eternity, just as the "Let there be" is conceived.

The planet from the Sanctum is an aspect in the "Let there be," which the primordial Wisdom formed and shaped in this way. This heavenly planet, which now moves on the path to the Kingdom of Peace, and from the Kingdom of Peace to the Sanctum, was the desired planet of a being from the Sanctum, which believed that it had to put through its wanting and desires.

The whole undertaking failed because of personal wanting and desires, which means: failed, exposing itself in a billionfold offense in space and time, with militant fighting, with murder, manslaughter, rape, extermination of whole tribes of people and much more.

Time has run out and the Satanist—thus called because of the root of his satanic demand—has capitulated.

The New Era up to the Kingdom of Peace and from the Kingdom of Peace to eternity, to the Sanctum, bears completion in the "Let there be."

Infinity receives further radiant garments, six mighty universes with the respective four associated planes of development, because the diversity of life has a corresponding inherent desire toward balance, or, for better understanding, a desire for a cradle.

The desire for balance or for a cradle contains in each case four planes of development from the ray of light of God, the Father-Mother-God, which follows the path of evolution according to the perpetual desire of the respective supporting pair of the corresponding universe, which is accompanied in love and care by the cherubim and seraphim, by the respective Cherub and Seraph of Order, of Will, of Earnestness, Kindness, Love and Meekness, and by the families of the respective regencies.

The corresponding universe of Wisdom has been following this path of evolution since the very beginning.

I, Christ, would now like to go as far as human beings can understand, in order to explain what it means to come home to the Kingdom of God, to the divine families—one can also say: to be eternally at home in the Father's house, in the community of all divine families in the Father-Mother-Being.

The path to the eternal Father's house begins—spoken with three dimensional words—on the lower levels.

As already indicated, from the depths of the innermost radiation of the planet Earth, the planet that belongs to the Kingdom of Peace is rising. In the soul realms and on the Earth among human beings, it makes itself more and more noticeable wherever it establishes the areas of incarnation on all continents. This draws through cities, villages, homesteads and hamlets, through all concentrations of human beings.

Not visible for the people, mighty incarnation areas with a differing light radiation emerge, which is, respectively, an indication of the type, of the progression of the incarnations.

If one wants to speak of colors, in terms of the light radiation of the incarnation areas, then it can be said: They go from light gray to medium gray to dark gray; from earth brown to black, or from sunny areas all the way to the transition onto the light-filled Christ-path, which no longer has any incarnations.

The person or soul on the brighter pathways suddenly feels as if enveloped in mist-like formations. In this state of consciousness, it hears aspects from nature or from its surrounding area of people and souls that live in the same state of consciousness. Very gradually, the communication among them begins. They understand each other and encourage each other, because the perception from the very basis of the soul becomes more and more heartfelt and familiar. The past, the sinful, the cruel time seems to be overcome. The people draw nearer and nearer to the Kingdom of Peace and try to order their lives in the spirit of community, to take care of nature together, but also of the animals, and to live together in an orderly way. Strangely, the diet is also quite different. One leads a different life through corresponding communication.

If the soul of a person walking the Christ-path now leaves its earthly body, then it may meet other beings from more light-filled realms, depending on the personal evolution of the soul.

A call resounds: "We know each other!" and the question is immediately added: "Where do you come from?"

A clear, trusting answer, of course, via the communication of sending and receiving:

"I come from the eternal homeland, from the Kingdom of God." And already it is done—the beings embrace each other.

The being that arrives now looks around, it is totally changed. The change is nothing new, it has always been a divine being, but now it has arrived from space and time, where it had a body of solid matter.

In his development, the person oriented himself to Christ, to the fullness of the law, which as a whole means: God in us, and we in God. The person learned to turn to God, to the kingdoms of nature and to the communicative behavior patterns with people, even if they were not always considerate. Likewise, he paid attention to everything that nature gives, including water and food.

After this path of refinement, it was easy, indeed, quickly possible, for the spirit being that had now arrived to feel the way it is now—a spirit being.

Spoken for the consciousness "world," now follows more insight into the cosmic event.

Like a stream from below, from the gloomy, gray, sorrowful world, innumerable animal species come in a kind of streams of mist into the light-filled realms, guided and supported by nature beings, and always under the guidance of the supporting pair of Wisdom. One can hardly believe with what alacrity the animal species remove themselves from their protective envelopment and walk or fly as if on their own toward the area that corresponds to their respective state of consciousness, just as they are still accustomed to doing.

In these and further cycles, beings released from their coarse-material bodies come, however, still somewhat shyly, until they see beings coming joyfully toward them. Very gradually the question forms, "Where do I come from, who am I?"

After brief moments, realization sets in and a communicative shiver permeated with joy reveals, "I have arrived, I am home!"

In these intimate, unifying glimpses of joy, the newly arrived beings recognize all that is around them, the eternal homeland, the extended family and among them the duals, who embrace their loved ones, all beings, the mature and the maturing—in human words: the adults and the children.

One single joyful stream of reunion, of fraternity, an indescribable joy!

Behold, the next wave of arrivals comes, led by the supporting pair of Wisdom and the nature beings. In this wave, there are plant species that never managed to blossom on the deeply fallen world spectacle. They still lay subdued in the Light-Ether, which the Satanist had insisted upon for himself.

With these plant species, which still hardly give off a ray of consciousness, the nature beings have the hardest time bringing them to the corresponding genus fields. But behold, the supporting pair of Wisdom knows immediately what to do. The

Cherub accompanies the stream of plant species, and the Seraph gathers the nature beings around. Together they pause. Suddenly, rays of light rise from the genus field, and the nature beings take care of the innumerable genus plants, which now take their place on the genus fields, which are also called the cradle for the nation of children.

But that is not enough:

As the streams come from below, from the gloomy harsh world, and gradually rise higher and higher, spirit beings develop and are received by their families.

Verily, the eternal homeland is opening up! Wherever one looks, there is the home, the law of love for God and neighbor.

The awareness of home opens, the eyes, the senses expand, a shudder draws through the spiritual body, an experience without end, there is no space, no time.

Eternity, of course, has many aspects, which the heavenly senses perceive only slowly and with caution.

Infinity, life, is everything in all things.

The diversity of life, infinity, cannot be described with the words of human beings.

We spirit beings are divine beings in infinity, but not God. Every divine being is spirit of His Spirit, God, and from Him, the All-One, a divine being, a spirit being.

We do not sow, we do not reap—we are.

The tasks of the divine beings, the spirit beings, are endlessly manifold, for which there are no human words.

Human beings and their words are exclusively oriented to the Earth. Words are shells in which lies what the person does not want to express or cannot express, because he lacks the appropriate words for this.

Human beings have no communication with the planets, although they once inhabited them, albeit with a corresponding finer-material body.

In terms of the earth itself, human beings have, for example, no communication with the grain that they sowed in the spring, at most, how it ripens and when they can cut it. In autumn, they bring the life into their barns. But that everything sends and that we could receive, they do not think about this. It is enough for them if the life brings a good profit.

If I, Christ, had to continue dictating to the instrument, I would come to meat production. The horrible suffering that takes place in the barns, on animal transporters, in the slaughterhouses and in the experimental institutions, I will not ask of My instrument, the prophetess of God, the interpreter for the Eternal Kingdom, except for one word—"cruel." The same is true regarding the suffering of all free animals in their various habitats.

That is the human being on this planet Earth, the only planet that still supports them, there is none other—only the wheel of the reincarnations on a thoroughly devastated planet.

Have human beings ever thought about how long their souls have been going through reincarnations?

Certainly not.

My answer is: Whether people believe in a soul with its soul core, also called soul spark, or not, after a certain time, the soul core, the core of being, moves away and goes on, on a path that the human being has imposed on it, but not with the soul burdened with suffering and agony.

The core of being indeed takes streams from its soul with it, but not for expiation—that takes place with reincarnation.

The whole thing also continues only for a while, then it is: earth to earth; the transformation changes the body into the corresponding substance, into finer-material up to fine-material; the material planet decreases, its state, as well, is transformed. With time—which means, in the times of times—everything becomes subject to transformation. Everything becomes again fine-material, creating and drawing primordial matter, which is already prepared for the next six mighty, unending spiritual universes. Each of these six emerging endless universes already has the corresponding structuring, based on its basic rays.

The Sanctum remains the center for all seven universes, which are mighty and infinite in their structure. The activity of the divine beings in the seven basic rays of the seven universes flows through the Sanctum and continues to build up with power and creative force.

As it is already written, each universe has its central sun and the seven basic rays that flow through all the others. This is also the symbiosis of unity—one serves the other.

The desire, the striving of a renegade being to provide proof to the Eternal of how HE should have done it better, not only went wrong, but went wrong from the ground up.

The Satanist, as the seven cherubim call him, wanted to create beings who beget themselves, a man with corresponding procreative possibilities, and a woman who receives the man's fluid from which a child should develop—which also took place.

However, the people became heavier and heavier, coarse-material, with flesh and blood, so that they could no longer move in the All, but became earthbound, as did their children.

The planet Earth is one planet among many. The All is filled with planets, all of it a loan from the Eternal to one spirit being—I call it as it is written in the Sanctum: "Satanist."

He wanted to prove that children come from two beings and that God, the Eternal All-One, is therefore, not the Father-Mother-God.

Because this endeavor and also other similar concepts did not succeed for him, he created a center, which put through his wanting and desires. These structures and still others fell deeper and deeper, because his experts of the Fall, who carried out his desires, became more and more attached to their bodies, that is, they became denser and denser in their physical structure.

This, in turn, meant that their residential planets could no longer support them and they had to leave them. They fell deeper and deeper.

The whole thing can be understood if one starts from conditions on the Earth. Everything that people transport into space that has no permanent propulsion falls back to Earth. Even the leaf that falls from the tree is proof. In this way, the whole Fall-system fell deeper and deeper.

That time contains a certain measure of time, which can be calculated and measured, clearly expresses: from—to.

The life of the individual human being is also conditioned by time—what then?

A person who does not believe in a soul speaks like the center of the evildoer: "Then it is over, earth to earth, dust to dust." Then, with so-called holy water, flesh and blood, that is, the deceased body, is often given to the earth.

Who can prove that after the last breath, life is actually over?

Revealed from the Eternal Kingdom: No energy is lost. The time "from—to" is merely a loan.

For the animals, for the entire plant world and also for the minerals, the stones, no matter how large the massif is, the following holds true: It is all a loan and thus, energy conditioned by time.

The same applies to the so-called "dead" human body, whether, as a human being, he believed in a soul or not.

If the deceased body did not have a soul, then it goes to the earth like all other deceased bodies; however, the soul of an ensouled human being draws out of the body, detaches itself from it and takes up the path that was already predetermined for it at the birth of the human being.

In those human beings who were born without a soul, their behavior, that is, their offence, remains stored in their so-called dead body. It is the same with those who let their soul become impoverished by the belief in the non-existence of God, except for the core of being of their soul, which extricates itself from the abuse, that is, from the burdened soul as such, and envelops itself with what the persons had in themselves as all-too-human aspects—however, not with the evil, which, as a sum of the whole, is also called criminal.

With this envelopment, the core of being takes the path that is determined for it. The heavy, that is, burdening, aspects, are taken along by the departed substance, the former human being, to reincarnation, in order to expiate them as a human being in another body.

The core of being takes the path to its destination, which is the Kingdom of Peace.

Thus, no being is lost; the core of being expiates the allocated lighter burdens of the soul and then enters the Kingdom of Peace and goes on to the Kingdom of Heaven.

From the Kingdom of Peace onward, the disembodied being becomes a spirit being, that is, the core of being again has its purpose from the Eternal Kingdom. The being is at home with the extended family and again fulfills the task that it has to fulfill according to its mentality.

The All-life continues, because, as already reported, the Light-Ether draws and creates further forms in six other creating, endless universes.

The seventh infinite universe is, as stated, the existing one of the divine Wisdom.

The Eternal Kingdom is the Eternal Kingdom.

There are now a total of seven unending universes with their respective prism suns, which are the All-unity in the composite of rays.

At the end of the text of the song of adoration of God, it says:

"O Christ, that Your name be imprinted,
deeply engraved in this mine heart!
May Your true love and brotherly kindness,
be stamped for always in heart and sense!
In word, in deed, in every being,
May it be Christ, and none other to be read."

The Christ of God closes His revelation with the words:

The Sanctum, the primordial seat of the Father-Mother-God, works above all.

Infinity is simply infinity, here can only be said with earthly words: The eternal Being is the infinity.

It is done.
It is over.
There is neither space nor time.
There is no more flesh and blood, no human beings and no human words.

It is done.
God is.